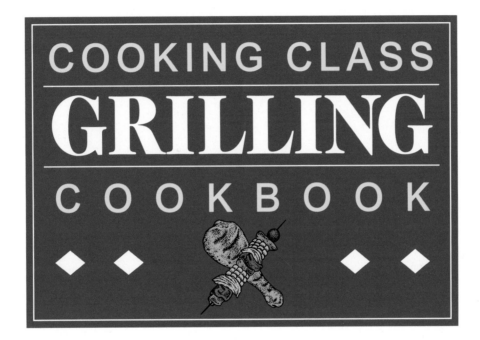

COOKING CLASS
GRILLING
COOKBOOK

PUBLICATIONS INTERNATIONAL, LTD.

Photography: Sacco Productions Limited, Chicago.

Pictured on the front cover *(clockwise from top left):* Buffalo Chicken Drumsticks *(page 72),* Seasoned Baby Back Ribs *(page 32)* and Hickory Beef Kabobs *(page 20).*
Pictured on the inside front cover: Grilled Beef Salad *(page 12).*
Pictured on the back cover: Barbecued Pork Tenderloin Sandwiches *(page 36).*

ISBN: 0-7853-0739-7

Manufactured in U.S.A.

8 7 6 5 4 3 2 1

CONTENTS

Fajitas with Avocado Salsa *(page 15)*

Grilled Shrimp Creole *(page 57)*

Grilled Cajun Potato Wedges *(page 84)*

CLASS NOTES

Cooking over an open fire is the oldest cooking technique known to man. Developed purely in a quest for survival, this ancient art has come a long way since then—new and innovative grilling and flavoring techniques have turned standard backyard fare into cookout cuisine. This tantalizing style of cooking with its mouthwatering aromas offers endless opportunities for both the novice and experienced pro. A simple review of the basics will ensure great success with all the delicious recipes in *Cooking Class Grilling*. With easy step-by-step instructions and helpful how-to photographs, your grill is sure to be fired up all summer—and possibly, all winter long!

CHOOSING A GRILL

Before you choose a grill, consider where you grill, what you'll be cooking, the seasons when you'll be grilling and the size of your budget. A small portable grill is fine if you usually barbecue smaller cuts of meat for a few people. For larger cuts of meat, bigger groups of people and year-round grilling, a large covered grill is worth the expense. Basic types of grills include gas, covered cooker and portable.

Gas Grill: Fast starts, accurate heat control, even cooking and year-round use make this the most convenient type of grill. Bottled gas heats a bed of lava rock or ceramic coals—no charcoal is required. Fat from the meat drips onto the lava rocks or coals and produces smoke for a grilled flavor. Hickory or fruitwood chips can be used to create the typical smoky flavor of charcoal.

Covered Cooker: Square, rectangular or kettle-shaped, this versatile covered grill lets you roast, steam, smoke or cook whole meals in any season of the year. Draft controls on the lid and base help control the temperature. Closing the dampers reduces the heat; opening them increases it. When the grill is covered, heat is reflected off the inside of the grill, cooking the food evenly and keeping it moist. When grilling without the cover, the coals are hotter since added air circulation promotes their burning.

Portable Grills: These include the familiar hibachi and small picnic grills. Portability and easy storage are their main advantage. When choosing a suitable portable grill, consider what would be best for your cooking and transporting needs, and make sure it is sturdy.

FIRE BUILDING

For safety's sake, make sure the grill is located on a solid surface, set away from shrubbery, grass and overhangs. Also, make sure the grill vents are not clogged with ashes before starting a fire. NEVER use gasoline or kerosene as a lighter fluid starter. Either one can cause an explosion. To get a sluggish fire going, do not add lighter fluid directly to hot coals. Instead, place two to three additional coals in a small metal can and add lighter fluid. Then stack them on the previously burning coals with barbecue or long-handled tongs and light with a match. These coals will restart the fire. Flare-ups blacken food and are a fire hazard; keep a water-filled spray bottle near the grill to quench them.

Remember that coals are hot (up to 1,000°F) and that the heat transfers to the barbecue grill, grid, tools and food. Always wear heavy-duty fireproof mitts when cooking and handling grill and tools.

The number of coals required for barbecuing depends on the size and type of grill and the amount of food to be prepared. Weather conditions also have an effect; strong winds, very cold temperatures or highly humid conditions increase the number of coals needed for a good fire. As a general rule, it takes about 30 coals to grill one pound of meat under optimum weather conditions.

To light a charcoal fire, arrange the coals in a pyramid shape about 20 to 30 minutes prior to cooking. The pyramid shape provides enough ventilation for the coals to catch. To start with lighter fluid, soak the coals with about ½ cup fluid. Wait one minute to allow the fluid to soak into the coals. Light with a match.

To start with an electric starter, nestle the starter in the center of coals. Plug the starter into a heavy-duty extension cord, then plug the cord into an outlet. After 8 to 10 minutes, when ash begins to form on the coals, unplug the starter and remove it. The electric starter will be very hot and should cool in a safe, heatproof place.

To start with a chimney starter, remove the grid from the grill; place the chimney starter in the base of grill. Crumble a few sheets of newspaper; place in the bottom portion of the chimney starter. Fill the top portion with coals. Light the newspaper. Do not disturb the starter; the coals will be ready in 20 to 30 minutes. Be sure to wear fireproof mitts when pouring the hot coals from the chimney starter into the base of the grill. This method is essentially failure-proof since it does not use starter fluid.

When the coals are ready, they will be about 80% ash gray during daylight and will glow at night. Spread the coals into a single layer with barbecue or long-handled tongs. To lower the cooking temperature, spread the coals farther apart or raise the grid. To raise the cooking temperature, either lower the grid or move the coals closer together and tap off the ash.

It is important to keep the grid, or cooking rack, clean and free of any bits of charred food. The easiest way is to scrub the grid with a stiff wire brush immediately after cooking, while the grid is still warm.

COOKING METHODS

Direct Cooking: The food is placed on the grid directly over the coals. Make sure there is enough charcoal in a single layer to extend 1 to 2 inches beyond the area of the food on the grill. This method is for quick-cooking foods, such as hamburgers, steaks and fish.

Indirect Cooking: The food is placed on the grid over a metal or disposable foil drip pan with the coals banked either to one side or on both sides of the pan. The drip pan keeps the grill clean and minimizes flare-ups. To cook with moist heat, add liquid to the drip pan during cooking if necessary. this method is best used for foods that require longer cooking time and even, less intense heat, such as roasts and whole chickens.

When barbecuing by indirect cooking for more than 45 minutes, add 4 to 9 coals around the outer edge of the fire just before you begin grilling. When these coals are ready, add them to the center of the fire as needed to maintain a constant temperature.

Here's how to determine the number of coals needed:

Coals Needed for Indirect Cooking, Covered Grill

Coals needed on each side of drip pan for cooking 45 to 50 minutes:

Diameter of Grill (inches)	Number of Coals
26¾	30
22½	25
18½	16
14	15

Coals needed to be added on each side of drip pan every 45 minutes for longer cooking:

Diameter of Grill (inches)	Number of Coals
26¾	9
22½	8
18½	5
14	4

CHECKING CHARCOAL TEMPERATURE

A quick, easy way to estimate the temperature of the coals is to cautiously hold your hand, palm-side down, about 4 inches above the coals. Count the number of seconds you can hold your hand in that position before the heat forces you to pull it away.

Seconds	Coal Temperature
2	hot, 375°F or more
3	medium-hot, 350° to 375°F
4	medium, 300° to 350°F
5	low, 200° to 300°F

FLAVORED SMOKE

Flavored smoke, a combination of heady aromas from hardwoods and fresh or dried herbs, imparts a special flavor to barbecued foods.

As a general rule, a little goes a long way. Added flavorings should complement, not overpower, food's natural taste. Always soak flavorings, such as wood chunks or chips, in water at least 20 minutes before adding to the coals so that they smolder and smoke, not burn. Small bunches of fresh or dried herbs soaked in water can also add fragrant flavor when sprinkled over hot coals. Rosemary, oregano and tarragon, for example, can be teamed with wood chips or simply used by themselves for a new taste.

For a different effect, try soaking wood chips and herbs in wine, rather than water. For poultry and seafood, use white wine with either basil, rosemary, tarragon, thyme or dill. For beef and pork, use red wine with either thyme, marjoram or bay leaves.

Many diverse woods are available for use on the grill in supermarkets, hardware stores and specialty stores. Only hardwoods or fruitwoods, such as hickory, oak, mesquite, pear or apple should be used to produce aromatic smoke. If you chip your own wood, never use softwoods, such as cedar, pine or spruce; these emit resins that can give food an unpleasant taste.

USING A GAS GRILL

Carefully follow the instructions in your owner's manual for lighting a gas grill. Once the grill is lit, turn on all burners to "high." The grill should be ready to use in about 10 minutes.

For direct cooking, the burners may be left at the "high" setting to sear the food, and then reduced immediately to "medium." Continue to cook at "medium" or "low." Gas grills cook the most evenly and with the fewest flare-ups at "medium" or "low," with temperatures in the 250° to 375°F range. This is equivalent to medium-hot to low for charcoal. If flare-ups are a problem, one or more of the burners can be turned to a lower setting.

For indirect cooking, preheat the grill as directed above. Turn the center burner to "off" and the two side burners to "medium." Place a metal or disposable foil drip pan directly on the lava rocks in the center of the grill. Place the food on the grill directly over the drip pan. If you wish to sear the food, first place it over a side burner, then move it to the center. For indirect cooking on a dual burner grill, turn one side of the grill to "off." Place the food on the unheated side of the grill, over the drip pan.

Do not use water to quench flare-ups on a gas grill. Close the hood and turn the heat down until the flaring subsides. Trimming as much fat as possible from the meat before grilling or using a drip pan also helps.

Although the distinctive smoky flavor of charcoal is missing on a gas grill, wood chips and chunks are great flavor alternatives. Most manufacturers advise against putting these directly on the lava rocks, since ash can clog the gas lines. Simply soak the chips or chunks for 20 minutes, drain and place in a metal or disposable foil drip pan. Poke several holes in the bottom of the pan and place it directly on the lava rocks. Preheat it with the grill.

DRY RUBS AND MARINADES

Dry rubs are seasoning blends rubbed onto meat before grilling and often include coarsely ground black or white pepper, paprika and garlic powder. Sometimes mustard, brown sugar and ground red pepper are used. Crushed herbs, such as sage, basil, thyme and oregano are other good choices.

Marinades add flavor and also moisten the surface of the meat to prevent it from drying out over the hot coals. Marinades include an acidic ingredient for tenderizing, such as wine, vinegar or lemon juice, combined with herbs, seasonings and oil. Fish and vegetables do not need tenderizing and should be marinated for only short periods of time. Beef, pork, lamb and chicken should be marinated for a few hours to overnight. Turn marinating foods occasionally to let the flavor infuse evenly. For safety, marinate all meats in the refrigerator. Because marinades contain an acid ingredient, marinating should be done in a glass, ceramic or stainless-steel container. The acid can cause a chemical reaction if marinating is done in an aluminum pan. Resealable plastic food storage bags are also great to hold foods as they marinate.

Reserve some of the marinade before adding the meat to use as a baste while the meat is cooking. A marinade drained from meat can also be used as a baste—just be sure to allow the meat to cook on the grill at least 5 minutes after the last application of marinade. You can also serve marinade that has been drained from the meat as a dipping sauce. However, follow food safety practices by placing the marinade in a small saucepan, bringing it to a full boil and boiling for at least 1 minute. These precautions are necessary to prevent the cooked food from becoming contaminated with bacteria from the raw meat present in the marinade.

TOOLS AND ACCESSORIES

These tools and accessories will make your barbecuing safer and more convenient.

Long-Handled Tongs, Basting Brush and Spatula: These are used to move hot coals and food around the grill, as well as for basting and turning foods. Select tools with long handles and hang them where you are working. You may want to purchase 2 pairs of tongs, 1 for coals and 1 for food.

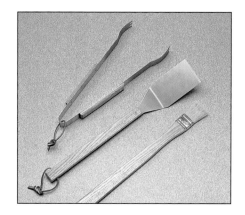

Meat Thermometers: The best way to judge the doneness of meat is with a high-quality meat thermometer. Prior to grilling, insert the thermometer into the center of the largest muscle of the meat with the point away from bone, fat or rotisserie rod. An instant-read thermometer gives an accurate reading within seconds of insertion, although it is not heatproof and should not be left in the meat during grilling.

Water Spritzer: To quench flare-ups when grilling with charcoal, keep a water-filled spray bottle near the barbecue.

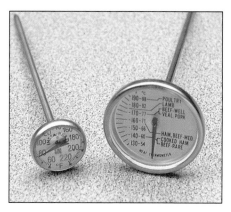

Heavy-Duty Mitts: You will prevent many burns by safeguarding your hands with heavy-duty fireproof mitts. Keep them close to the barbecue so they are always handy.

Aluminum Foil: Some vegetables are enclosed in aluminum foil packets before placing either directly on the coals or on the grid to cook. To ensure even cooking without any leakage, use the Drugstore Wrap technique. Place the food in the center of an oblong piece of heavy-duty foil, leaving at least a 2-inch border around the food. Bring the 2 long sides together above the food; fold down in a series of locked folds, allowing for heat circulation and expansion.

Fold the short ends up and over again. Crimp closed to seal the foil packet.

Metal or Disposable Foil Drip Pans: A drip pan placed beneath grilling meats prevents flare-ups. The pan should be 1½ inches deep and extend about 3 inches beyond either end of the meat. The juices that collect in the drip pan may be used for a sauce or gravy. Bring drippings to a boil before using.

Hinged Wire Baskets: These baskets are designed to hold fish fillets and other irregularly shaped foods. They also facilitate turning for smaller pieces of meat that are too small for the cooking grid or would be awkward to handle individually.

Rib Racks: Rib racks increase the grill's cooking capacity by standing slabs of ribs at an angle to the heat source.

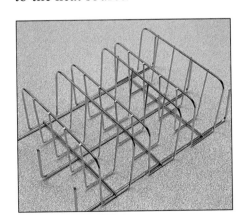

Skewers: Made of either metal or bamboo, skewers are indispensable for kabobs. Bamboo skewers should be soaked in water at least 20 minutes before grilling to prevent the bamboo from burning.

BARBECUE TIPS

• Always use tongs or a spatula when handling meat. Piercing meat with a fork allows delicious juices to escape and makes meat less moist.

• If you partially cook food in the microwave or on the range, *immediately* finish cooking the food on the grill. Do not refrigerate or let stand at room temperature before cooking on the grill.

• Wash all utensils, cutting boards and containers with hot soapy water after they have been in contact with uncooked meat.

• Always serve cooked food from the grill on a clean plate, not one that held the raw food.

• In hot weather, food should never sit out for over 1 hour. Remember, keep hot foods hot and cold foods cold.

• The cooking rack, or grid, should be kept clean and free of any bits of charred food. The easiest way is to scrub the grid with a stiff wire brush while it is still warm.

• Watch foods carefully during grilling. Total cooking time will vary with the type of food, position on the grill, weather, temperature of the coals and the degree of doneness you desire.

• Set a timer to remind you when it's time to check the food on the grill.

• Store charcoal in a dry place. Charcoal absorbs moisture readily and won't burn well if it is damp.

• Top and bottom vents should be open before starting a charcoal grill and while cooking. Close vents when cooking is finished to extinguish the coals.

• For proper air flow in a charcoal grill, remove accumulated ashes from the bottom before starting the fire. Since charcoal requires oxygen to burn, anything blocking the vents will reduce the heat generated from the coals.

• Extend the life of your charcoal grill by thoroughly cleaning it once a year. Discard accumulated ashes and remove the grid and charcoal grates. Spray the porcelain surface with oven cleaner and let stand until the accumulated grease is softened. Wipe out with paper towels. Wash with a mild detergent and water; rinse and wipe dry.

• A vinyl or plastic grill cover is an inexpensive way to protect your grill from winter's harsh elements. It will ward off rust while adding years to the life of the grill.

Grilled Beef Salad

Assorted greens such as
   romaine, red leaf and Bibb
1 large tomato
   Fresh basil leaves
1 red onion
½ cup mayonnaise
2 tablespoons cider vinegar or
   white wine vinegar
1 tablespoon spicy brown
   mustard
2 cloves garlic, minced (technique
   on page 26)
½ teaspoon sugar
1 pound boneless beef top sirloin
   steak, cut 1 inch thick
½ teaspoon salt
½ teaspoon pepper
½ cup purchased herb or garlic
   croutons
   Additional pepper (optional)

1. Wash greens in several changes of cold water. Drain well and pat dry with paper towels to remove excess moisture, if necessary. Or, spin in salad spinner to remove moisture.

2. Discard any wilted or bruised leaves. Cut or tear off stems if they are woody. Tear enough lettuce into bite-sized pieces to measure 6 cups. Set aside.

3. To seed tomato, cut tomato in half horizontally. Hold each tomato half over bowl, cut-side down, and squeeze to remove seeds. Coarsely chop tomato with chef's knife. Set aside.

4. Layer basil leaves with largest leaf on bottom, then roll up jelly-roll style. Slice basil roll into very thin slices; separate into strips. Slice enough leaves to measure ⅓ cup. Set aside.

continued on page 14

Step 1. Spinning greens in salad spinner.

Step 2. Measuring lettuce pieces.

Step 3. Squeezing tomato half to remove seeds.

Grilled Beef Salad, continued

5. To prepare onion, slice off stem and root end; discard. Peel away skin. Cut onion crosswise into thin slices. Separate 2 slices into rings for recipe; reserve remaining onion for other uses.

6. Prepare barbecue grill for direct cooking.

7. While coals are heating, combine mayonnaise, vinegar, mustard, garlic and sugar in small bowl; mix well. Cover and refrigerate until serving.

8. Toss together greens, tomato, basil and onion rings in large bowl; cover and refrigerate until serving.

9. Sprinkle both sides of steak with salt and ½ teaspoon pepper. Place steak on grid. Grill steak, on covered grill, over medium-hot coals 10 minutes for medium-rare or until desired doneness is reached, turning halfway through grilling time.

10. Transfer steak to carving board. Slice in half lengthwise; carve crosswise into thin slices.

11. Add steak and croutons to bowl with greens; toss well. Add mayonnaise mixture; toss until well coated. Serve with additional pepper.

Makes 4 servings

Step 6. Briquets arranged in grill for direct cooking.

Step 8. Tossing together greens, tomato, basil and onion rings.

Step 9. Turning steak halfway through grilling time.

Fajitas with Avocado Salsa

1 to 2 fresh or drained, bottled jalapeño peppers
1 beef flank steak (1¼ to 1½ pounds)
¼ cup tequila or nonalcoholic beer
3 tablespoons fresh lime juice (technique on page 39)
2 large cloves garlic, minced (technique on page 26)
1 large red bell pepper
1 large green bell pepper Avocado Salsa (page 16)
8 flour tortillas (6- to 7-inch diameter)
4 slices red onion, cut ¼ inch thick (technique on page 36)

1. Slit jalapeños* open lengthwise using scissors or knife. Under cold running water, carefully pull out and discard the seeds and veins. Rinse jalapeños well and drain; pat dry with paper towels. Mince enough jalapeños to measure 1 tablespoon.

2. Place steak in large resealable plastic food storage bag. Combine tequila, lime juice, jalapeños and garlic in small bowl; pour over steak. Seal bag tightly, turning to coat. Marinate in refrigerator 1 to 4 hours, turning once.

3. Rinse bell peppers under cold running water. To seed peppers, stand on end on cutting board. Cut off sides into 4 lengthwise slices with utility knife. (Cut close to, but not through, stem.) Discard stem and seeds. Scrape out any remaining seeds. Rinse inside of peppers under cold running water. Set aside.

4. Prepare barbecue grill for direct cooking.

5. Meanwhile, prepare Avocado Salsa.

6. Wrap tortillas in heavy-duty foil using Drugstore Wrap technique. (Technique on page 10.)

*Jalapeño peppers can sting and irritate the skin; wear rubber gloves when handling peppers and do not touch eyes. Wash your hands after handling peppers.

continued on page 16

Step 1. Removing seeds and veins from jalapeño pepper.

Step 3. Cutting sides off bell pepper.

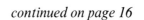

7. Drain steak; discard marinade. Place steak, bell peppers and onion slices on grid. Grill, on covered grill, over medium-hot coals 14 to 18 minutes for medium or until desired doneness is reached, turning steak, bell peppers and onion slices halfway through grilling time. Place tortilla packet on grid during last 5 to 7 minutes of grilling; turn halfway through grilling time to heat through.

8. Transfer steak to carving board. Carve steak across the grain into thin slices. Slice bell peppers into thin strips. Separate onion slices into rings. Divide among tortillas; roll up and top with Avocado Salsa.   *Makes 4 servings*

Avocado Salsa

1 ripe large avocado
1 large tomato, seeded and diced (technique on page 12)
3 tablespoons chopped cilantro
1 tablespoon vegetable oil
1 tablespoon fresh lime juice (technique on page 39)
2 teaspoons minced fresh or drained, bottled jalapeño peppers (technique on page 15)
1 clove garlic, minced (technique on page 26)
½ teaspoon salt

1. To prepare avocado, place avocado on cutting board. Insert utility knife into stem end of avocado; slice in half lengthwise to the pit, turning avocado while slicing. Remove knife blade; twist both halves to pull apart. Press knife blade into pit; twist knife to pull pit from avocado.

2. Scoop avocado flesh out of shells with large spoon; place on cutting board. Coarsely chop avocado flesh into ½-inch cubes. Transfer to medium bowl.

3. Gently stir in tomato, cilantro, oil, lime juice, jalapeños, garlic and salt until well combined. Let stand at room temperature while grilling steak. Cover; refrigerate if preparing in advance. Bring to room temperature before serving.   *Makes about 1½ cups*

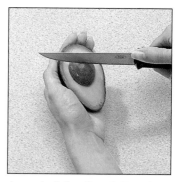

Avocado Salsa: Step 1. Pressing knife blade into pit of avocado.

Avocado Salsa: Step 2. Scooping avocado flesh out of shells.

Mexicali Burgers

GUACAMOLE
- **1 ripe avocado, pitted (technique on page 16)**
- **1 tablespoon purchased salsa or picante sauce**
- **1 teaspoon fresh lime or lemon juice (technique on page 39)**
- **¼ teaspoon garlic salt**

BURGERS
- **Tortilla chips**
- **⅓ cup purchased salsa or picante sauce**
- **1 pound ground chuck**
- **3 tablespoons finely chopped cilantro**
- **2 tablespoons grated onion (technique on page 20)**
- **1 teaspoon ground cumin**
- **4 slices Monterey Jack or Cheddar cheese**
- **4 Kaiser rolls or hamburger buns, split**
- **Lettuce leaves (optional)**
- **Sliced tomatoes (optional)**

1. Prepare barbecue grill with rectangular metal or foil drip pan. Bank briquets on either side of drip pan for indirect cooking.

2. Meanwhile, to prepare Guacamole, scoop avocado flesh out of shells with large spoon; place in medium bowl. Mash roughly with fork or wooden spoon, leaving avocado slightly chunky.

3. Stir in 1 tablespoon salsa, lime juice and garlic salt. Let stand at room temperature while grilling burgers. Cover; refrigerate if preparing in advance. Bring to room temperature before serving.

4. Place tortilla chips in large resealable plastic food storage bag; seal. Finely crush chips with mallet or rolling pin to measure ⅓ cup.

5. Combine ⅓ cup salsa, beef, tortilla chips, cilantro, onion and cumin in medium bowl. Mix lightly but thoroughly. Shape mixture into four ½-inch-thick burgers, 4 inches in diameter.

6. Place burgers on grid. Grill burgers, on covered grill, over medium coals 8 to 10 minutes for medium or until desired doneness is reached, turning halfway through grilling time.

7. Place 1 slice cheese on each burger to melt during last 1 to 2 minutes of grilling. If desired, place rolls, cut-side down, on grid to toast lightly during last 1 to 2 minutes of grilling. Place burgers between rolls; top burgers with Guacamole. Serve with lettuce and tomatoes. *Makes 4 servings*

Step 2. Mashing avocado until slightly chunky.

Step 4. Crushing tortilla chips.

Step 5. Shaping beef mixture into burgers.

Grilled Meat Loaf

1 small onion
1½ pounds ground chuck or ground sirloin
½ cup seasoned dry bread crumbs
⅔ cup chili sauce, divided
1 egg
½ teaspoon pepper
¼ teaspoon salt
2 tablespoons packed light brown sugar
1 tablespoon spicy brown or Dijon-style mustard

1. Prepare barbecue grill for direct cooking.

2. Meanwhile, to prepare onion, slice off stem and root end; discard. Peel away skin. Grate onion using the largest holes on box-shaped grater. Grate enough onion to measure ⅓ cup.

3. Combine beef, bread crumbs, onion, ⅓ cup chili sauce, egg, pepper and salt in large bowl; mix well. On cutting board or cookie sheet, shape mixture into an oval loaf 1½ inches thick, about 9 inches long and 5 inches wide.

4. Combine remaining ⅓ cup chili sauce, sugar and mustard in small bowl; mix well. Set aside.

5. Place meat loaf on grid. Grill meat loaf, on covered grill, over medium-hot coals 10 minutes. Carefully turn meat loaf over using 2 large spatulas.

6. Brush chili sauce mixture over top of meat loaf. Continue to grill, covered, 10 to 12 minutes for medium-well or until desired doneness is reached. (If desired, insert instant-read thermometer* into center of thickest part of meat loaf. Thermometer should register 160°F for medium-well.) Let stand 10 minutes before slicing. Serve with mashed potatoes and peas and carrots, if desired.

Makes 4 to 6 servings

*Do not leave instant-read thermometer in meat loaf during grilling since the thermometer is not heatproof.

Step 2. Grating onion using largest holes on box-shaped grater.

Step 3. Shaping beef mixture into an oval loaf.

Step 5. Carefully turning meat loaf over with 2 large spatulas.

Hickory Beef Kabobs

2 ears fresh corn,* shucked and cleaned (technique on page 40)
1 pound boneless beef top sirloin or tenderloin steak, cut into 1¼-inch pieces
1 red or green bell pepper, cut into 1-inch squares
1 small red onion, cut into ½-inch wedges
½ cup beer or nonalcoholic beer
½ cup chili sauce
1 teaspoon dry mustard
2 cloves garlic, minced (technique on page 26)
1½ cups hickory chips
4 metal skewers (12 inches long)
3 cups hot cooked white rice
¼ cup chopped fresh parsley
Fresh parsley sprigs and plum tomatoes for garnish

*Four small ears frozen corn, thawed, can be substituted for fresh corn.

1. Place corn on cutting board. Cut crosswise with chef's knife into 1-inch pieces.

2. Place beef, bell pepper, onion and corn in large resealable plastic food storage bag. Combine beer, chili sauce, mustard and garlic in small bowl; pour over beef and vegetables. Seal bag tightly, turning to coat. Marinate in refrigerator at least 1 hour or up to 8 hours, turning occasionally.

3. Prepare barbecue grill for direct cooking.

4. Meanwhile, cover hickory chips with cold water; soak 20 minutes.

5. Drain beef and vegetables; reserve marinade. Alternately thread beef and vegetables onto skewers. Brush with reserved marinade.

6. Drain hickory chips; sprinkle over coals. Place kabobs on grid. Grill kabobs, on covered grill, over medium-hot coals 5 minutes. Brush with reserved marinade; turn and brush again. Discard remaining marinade. Continue to grill, covered, 5 to 7 minutes for medium or until desired doneness is reached.

7. Combine rice and chopped parsley; serve kabobs over rice mixture. Garnish, if desired.

Makes 4 servings

Step 1. Cutting corn crosswise into 1-inch pieces.

Step 3. Briquets arranged in grill for direct cooking.

Step 5. Alternately threading beef and vegetables onto skewers.

Korean Beef Short Ribs

1 tablespoon sesame seeds
6 to 8 green onions
2½ pounds flanken-style beef short
   ribs, cut ⅜ to ½ inch thick*
¼ cup soy sauce
¼ cup water
1 tablespoon sugar
2 teaspoons Oriental sesame oil
2 teaspoons grated fresh ginger
   (technique on page 62)
2 cloves garlic, minced (technique
   on page 26)
½ teaspoon pepper

*Flanken-style ribs may be ordered from
your meat retailer. They are cross-cut
short ribs sawed through the bones, ⅜- to
½-inch thick.

1. To toast sesame seeds, spread seeds in large, dry skillet. Shake skillet over medium-low heat until seeds begin to pop and turn golden, about 3 minutes. Set aside.

2. Rinse green onions under cold running water; pat dry with paper towels. Cut off root ends; discard. Finely chop enough green onions with tops to measure ¼ cup.

3. Place ribs in large resealable plastic food storage bag. Combine soy sauce, water, green onions, sugar, oil, ginger, garlic and pepper in small bowl; pour over ribs. Seal bag tightly, turning to coat. Marinate in refrigerator at least 4 hours or up to 24 hours, turning occasionally.

4. Prepare barbecue grill for direct cooking.

5. Drain ribs; reserve marinade. Place ribs on grid. Grill ribs, on covered grill, over medium-hot coals 5 minutes. Brush tops lightly with reserved marinade; turn and brush again. Discard remaining marinade. Continue to grill, covered, 5 to 6 minutes for medium or until desired doneness is reached. Sprinkle with sesame seeds. *Makes 4 to 6 servings*

Step 1. Shaking skillet until sesame seeds begin to pop and turn golden.

Step 2. Finely chopping green onions.

Step 3. Pouring marinade over ribs.

Peppered Beef Rib Roast

1½ tablespoons black peppercorns
2 cloves garlic
1 boneless beef rib roast (2½ to 3 pounds), well trimmed
¼ cup Dijon-style mustard
¾ cup sour cream
2 tablespoons prepared horseradish
1 tablespoon balsamic vinegar
½ teaspoon sugar

1. Prepare barbecue grill with rectangular metal or foil drip pan. Bank briquets on either side of drip pan for indirect cooking.

2. Meanwhile, to crack peppercorns, place peppercorns in heavy, small resealable plastic food storage bag. Squeeze out excess air; seal bag tightly. Pound peppercorns using flat side of meat mallet or rolling pin until cracked. Set aside.

3. To mince garlic, trim off ends of garlic cloves. Slightly crush cloves under flat side of chef's knife blade; peel away skin. Chop garlic with chef's knife until garlic is in uniform fine pieces.

4. Pat roast dry with paper towels. Combine mustard and garlic in small bowl; spread with spatula over top and sides of roast. Sprinkle pepper over mustard mixture.

5. Insert meat thermometer into center of thickest part of roast. Place roast, pepper-side up, on grid directly over drip pan. Grill roast, on covered grill, over medium coals 1 hour to 1 hour 10 minutes or until thermometer registers 150°F for medium-rare or until desired doneness is reached, adding 4 to 9 briquets to both sides of the fire after 45 minutes to maintain medium coals.

6. Meanwhile, combine sour cream, horseradish, vinegar and sugar in small bowl; mix well. Cover; refrigerate until serving.

7. Transfer roast to carving board; tent with foil. Let stand 5 to 10 minutes before carving. Serve with horseradish sauce.

Makes 6 to 8 servings

Step 2. Pounding peppercorns with meat mallet until cracked.

Step 3. Crushing garlic clove to remove peel.

Step 4. Spreading mustard mixture over top and sides of roast.

Calypso Pork Chops

1 ripe medium papaya
1 small piece fresh ginger
1 teaspoon paprika
½ teaspoon dried thyme leaves
¼ teaspoon salt
¼ teaspoon ground allspice
4 center-cut pork loin chops
    (about 1½ pounds), cut ¾ inch
    thick
5 tablespoons fresh lime juice,
    divided (technique on page 39)
2 tablespoons plus 1½ teaspoons
    seeded, chopped jalapeño
    peppers,* divided (technique
    on page 15)
1 tablespoon vegetable oil
1 teaspoon sugar
¼ cup finely diced red bell pepper
    Additional chopped jalapeño
    pepper for garnish

*Jalapeño peppers can sting and irritate the skin; wear rubber gloves when handling peppers and do not touch eyes. Wash your hands after handling peppers.

1. To prepare papaya, remove peel with paring knife or vegetable peeler. To seed papaya, slice in half lengthwise. Scrape out seeds with spoon; discard. Chop papaya flesh into ¼-inch pieces. Chop enough papaya to measure 1½ cups. Set aside.

2. To grate ginger, remove tough outer skin with sharp knife or vegetable peeler. Grate ginger using ginger grater or finest side of box-shaped grater. Grate enough ginger to measure 1½ teaspoons. Set aside.

3. Combine paprika, thyme, salt and allspice in small bowl; rub over both sides of pork chops with fingers. Place chops in large resealable plastic food storage bag.

4. Combine 3 tablespoons lime juice, 2 tablespoons jalapeños, oil, 1 teaspoon ginger and sugar in small bowl; pour over chops. Seal bag tightly, turning to coat. Marinate in refrigerator 1 to 2 hours.

5. Combine papaya, bell pepper, remaining 2 tablespoons lime juice, remaining 1½ teaspoons jalapeños and remaining ½ teaspoon ginger in another small bowl; cover and refrigerate until serving.

6. Prepare barbecue grill for direct cooking.

7. Meanwhile, drain chops; discard marinade. Place chops on grid. Grill chops, on covered grill, over medium coals 10 to 12 minutes or until pork is juicy and barely pink in center, turning halfway through grilling time. Serve chops topped with papaya mixture. Garnish, if desired. *Makes 4 servings*

Step 1. Scraping seeds out of papaya.

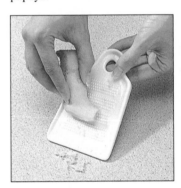

Step 2. Grating fresh ginger.

Step 3. Rubbing seasoning mixture over pork chops.

Brats 'n' Beer

1 can or bottle (12 ounces) beer (not dark) or nonalcoholic beer
4 fresh bratwurst (about 1 pound)
1 large sweet or Spanish onion (about ½ pound), thinly sliced and separated into rings (technique on page 14)
1 tablespoon olive or vegetable oil
¼ teaspoon salt
¼ teaspoon pepper
4 hot dog rolls, preferably bakery-style or onion, split
Coarse-grain or sweet-hot mustard (optional)
Drained sauerkraut (optional)

1. Prepare barbecue grill for direct cooking.

2. Pour beer into heavy medium saucepan with ovenproof handle. (If not ovenproof, wrap heavy-duty foil around handle.) Set saucepan on one side of grid.

3. Pierce each bratwurst in several places with tip of sharp knife. Carefully add bratwurst to beer; simmer, on uncovered grill, over medium coals 15 minutes, turning once.*

4. Meanwhile, place onion rings on 18×14-inch sheet of heavy-duty foil. Drizzle with oil; sprinkle with salt and pepper. Close foil using Drugstore Wrap technique. (Technique on page 10.) Place on grid next to saucepan. Grill onions, on uncovered grill, 10 to 15 minutes or until onions are tender.

5. Transfer bratwurst with tongs to grid; remove saucepan using heavy-duty mitt. Discard beer. Grill bratwurst, on covered grill, 9 to 10 minutes or until browned and cooked through, turning halfway through grilling time.

6. If desired, place rolls, cut-side down, on grid to toast lightly during last 1 to 2 minutes of grilling. Place bratwurst in rolls. Open foil packet carefully. Top each bratwurst with onions. Serve with mustard and sauerkraut.

Makes 4 servings

*If desired, bratwurst may be simmered on rangetop. Pour beer into medium saucepan. Bring to a boil over medium-high heat. Carefully add bratwurst to beer. Reduce heat to low and simmer, uncovered, 15 minutes, turning once.

Step 3. Adding bratwurst to beer.

Step 5. Transferring bratwurst to grid.

Seasoned Baby Back Ribs

1 tablespoon paprika
1½ teaspoons garlic salt
1 teaspoon celery salt
½ teaspoon black pepper
¼ teaspoon ground red pepper
4 pounds pork baby back ribs,
   cut into 3- to 4-rib portions,
   well trimmed
Barbecue Sauce (recipe
   follows)
Rib rack (optional)
Orange peel for garnish

1. Preheat oven to 350°F.

2. For seasoning rub, combine paprika, garlic salt, celery salt, black pepper and ground red pepper in small bowl. Rub over all surfaces of ribs with fingers.

3. Place ribs in foil-lined shallow roasting pan. Bake 30 minutes.

4. Meanwhile, prepare barbecue grill for direct cooking.

5. While coals are heating, prepare Barbecue Sauce.

6. Transfer ribs to rib rack set on grid. Or, place ribs directly on grid. Grill ribs, on covered grill, over medium coals 10 minutes.

7. Remove ribs from rib rack with tongs; brush with half the Barbecue Sauce evenly over both sides of ribs. Return ribs to rib rack. Continue to grill, covered, 10 minutes or until ribs are tender and browned. Serve with reserved sauce. Garnish, if desired.

Makes 6 servings

Step 2. Rubbing spice mixture over ribs.

Step 7. Brushing ribs with Barbecue Sauce.

Barbecue Sauce

½ cup ketchup
⅓ cup packed light brown sugar
1 tablespoon cider vinegar
2 teaspoons Worcestershire sauce
2 teaspoons soy sauce

Combine ketchup, sugar, vinegar, Worcestershire sauce and soy sauce in glass measuring cup or small bowl. Reserve half of sauce for serving.

Makes about ⅔ cup

Barbecue Sauce: Reserving half of sauce for serving.

Grilled Pork and Potatoes Vesuvio

1 center-cut boneless pork loin
    roast (1½ pounds), well
    trimmed
½ cup dry white wine
2 tablespoons olive oil
4 cloves garlic, minced, divided
    (technique on page 26)
1½ to 2 pounds small red potatoes
    (about 1½ inches in diameter),
    scrubbed
6 metal skewers (12 inches long)
6 lemon wedges
    Salt (optional)
    Pepper (optional)
¼ cup chopped fresh Italian or
    curly leaf parsley
1 teaspoon finely grated lemon
    peel

1. Cut pork into 1-inch cubes. Place pork in large resealable plastic food storage bag. Combine wine, oil and 3 cloves minced garlic in small bowl; pour over pork.

2. Place potatoes in single layer in microwave-safe dish. Pierce each potato with tip of sharp knife. Microwave at HIGH (100% power) 6 to 7 minutes or until almost tender when pierced with fork. (Or, place potatoes in large saucepan. Cover with cold water. Bring to a boil over high heat. Simmer about 12 minutes or until almost tender when pierced with fork.) Immediately rinse with cold water; drain. Add to pork in bag. Seal bag tightly, turning to coat. Marinate in refrigerator at least 2 hours or up to 8 hours, turning occasionally.

3. Prepare barbecue grill for direct cooking.

4. Meanwhile, drain pork mixture; discard marinade. Alternately thread about 3 pork cubes and 2 potatoes onto each skewer. Place 1 lemon wedge on end of each skewer. Sprinkle salt and pepper over pork and potatoes.

5. Place skewers on grid. Grill skewers, on covered grill, over medium coals 14 to 16 minutes or until pork is juicy and barely pink in center and potatoes are tender, turning halfway through grilling time.

6. Remove skewers from grill. Combine parsley, lemon peel and remaining minced garlic clove in small bowl. Sprinkle over pork and potatoes. Squeeze lemon wedges over pork and potatoes. *Makes 6 servings*

Step 4. Alternately threading pork and potatoes onto skewers.

Step 6. Sprinkling parsley mixture over pork and potatoes.

Barbecued Pork Tenderloin Sandwiches

1 clove garlic
1 large red onion
½ cup ketchup
⅓ cup packed brown sugar
2 tablespoons bourbon or whiskey (optional)
1 tablespoon Worcestershire sauce
½ teaspoon dry mustard
¼ teaspoon ground red pepper
2 whole pork tenderloins (about ¾ pound each), well trimmed
6 hoagie rolls or Kaiser rolls, split

1. Prepare barbecue grill for direct cooking.

2. To mince garlic, trim off ends of garlic clove. Slightly crush clove under flat side of chef's knife blade; peel away skin. Chop garlic with chef's knife until garlic is in uniform fine pieces. Set aside.

3. Meanwhile, to slice onion, slice off stem and root end; discard. Peel away skin. Cut onion crosswise into six ¼-inch-thick slices. Set aside.

4. Combine ketchup, sugar, bourbon, Worcestershire sauce, mustard, ground red pepper and garlic in small, heavy saucepan with ovenproof handle; mix well. (If not ovenproof, wrap heavy-duty foil around handle.)

continued on page 38

Step 1. Briquets arranged in grill for direct cooking.

Step 2. Crushing garlic clove to remove peel.

Step 3. Cutting onion crosswise into ¼-inch-thick slices.

Barbecued Pork Tenderloin Sandwiches, continued

5. Set saucepan on one side of grid.* Place tenderloins on center of grid. Grill tenderloins, on uncovered grill, over medium-hot coals 8 minutes. Simmer sauce 5 minutes or until thickened, stirring occasionally.

6. Turn tenderloins with tongs; continue to grill, uncovered, 5 minutes. Add onion slices to grid. Set aside half of sauce; reserve. Brush tenderloins and onions with a portion of remaining sauce.

7. Continue to grill, uncovered, 7 to 10 minutes or until pork is juicy and barely pink in center, brushing with remaining sauce and turning onions and tenderloins halfway through grilling time. (If desired, insert instant-read thermometer** into center of thickest part of tenderloins. Thermometer should register 160°F.)

8. Carve tenderloins crosswise into thin slices; separate onion slices into rings. Divide meat and onion rings among rolls; drizzle with reserved sauce.

Makes 6 servings

*If desired, sauce may be prepared on rangetop. Combine ketchup, sugar, bourbon, Worcestershire sauce, mustard, ground red pepper and garlic in small saucepan. Bring to a boil over medium-high heat. Reduce heat to low and simmer, uncovered, 5 minutes or until thickened, stirring occasionally.

**Do not leave instant-read thermometer in tenderloins during grilling since the thermometer is not heatproof.

Step 6. Brushing tenderloins and onions with portion of sauce.

Step 7. Inserting instant-read thermometer into thickest part of tenderloin.

Step 8. Carving tenderloins crosswise into thin slices.

Southwestern Lamb Chops with Charred Corn Relish

2 large limes
4 lamb shoulder or blade chops
(about 2 pounds), cut ¾ inch
thick, well trimmed
¼ cup vegetable oil
1 tablespoon chili powder
2 cloves garlic, minced (technique
on page 26)
1 teaspoon ground cumin
¼ teaspoon ground red pepper
Charred Corn Relish (page 40)
2 tablespoons chopped cilantro
Hot pepper jelly (optional)

1. To juice limes, cut limes in half on cutting board; with tip of knife, remove any visible seeds.

2. Using citrus reamer or squeezing tightly with hand, squeeze juice from limes into small glass or bowl. Remove any remaining seeds from juice. Squeeze enough juice to measure ¼ cup.

3. Place chops in large resealable plastic food storage bag. Combine oil, lime juice, chili powder, garlic, cumin and ground red pepper in small bowl; mix well. Reserve 3 tablespoons mixture for Charred Corn Relish; cover and refrigerate. Pour remaining mixture over chops. Seal bag tightly, turning to coat. Marinate in refrigerator at least 8 hours or overnight, turning occasionally.

4. Prepare barbecue grill for direct cooking.

5. Meanwhile, prepare Charred Corn Relish.

6. Drain chops; discard marinade from bag. Place chops on grid. Grill chops, on covered grill, over medium coals 13 to 15 minutes for medium or until desired doneness is reached, turning halfway through grilling time. Sprinkle with cilantro. Serve with Charred Corn Relish and hot pepper jelly.

Makes 4 servings

continued on page 40

Step 1. Removing seeds from lime.

Step 2. Squeezing juice from lime.

Charred Corn Relish

2 large or 3 small ears fresh corn
½ cup diced red bell pepper
¼ cup chopped cilantro
3 tablespoons reserved lime mixture

1. To shuck corn, pull outer husk from top to base of each ear of corn. Snap off husks and stem at base.

2. Strip away silk from corn by hand.

3. Remove any remaining silk with dry vegetable brush. Trim any blemishes from corn and rinse under cold running water.

4. Place corn on grid. Grill corn, on covered grill, over medium coals 10 to 12 minutes or until charred, turning occasionally. Cool to room temperature.

5. Holding tip of 1 ear, stand upright on its stem end in medium bowl. Cut down the sides of cob with paring knife, releasing kernels without cutting into cob.

6. Press down along each cob with dull edge of utility knife to release any remaining corn and liquid.

7. Add bell pepper, cilantro and reserved lime mixture to corn; mix well. Let stand at room temperature while grilling chops. Cover; refrigerate if preparing in advance. Bring to room temperature before serving.

Makes about 1½ cups

Charred Corn Relish: Step 1. Snapping husk and stem at base of corn.

Charred Corn Relish: Step 2. Stripping away silk from corn.

Charred Corn Relish: Step 5. Cutting down sides of cob to release kernels.

Mint Marinated Racks of Lamb

2 whole racks (6 ribs each) loin lamb chops (about 3 pounds), well trimmed
1 cup dry red wine
½ cup chopped fresh mint leaves (optional)
3 cloves garlic, minced (technique on page 26)
¼ cup Dijon-style mustard
2 tablespoons chopped fresh mint leaves *or* 2 teaspoons dried mint leaves, crushed
⅔ cup dry bread crumbs

1. Place lamb in large resealable plastic food storage bag. Combine wine, ½ cup mint and garlic in small bowl. Pour over chops. Seal bag tightly, turning to coat. Marinate in refrigerator at least 2 hours or up to 4 hours, turning occasionally.

2. Prepare barbecue grill for direct cooking.

3. Meanwhile, drain lamb; discard marinade. Pat lamb dry with paper towels. Place lamb in shallow glass dish or on cutting board. Combine mustard and 2 tablespoons mint in small bowl; spread with spatula over meaty side of lamb. Pat bread crumbs evenly over mustard mixture.

4. Place lamb, crumb-side down, on grid. Grill lamb, on covered grill, over medium coals 10 minutes. Carefully turn with tongs. Continue to grill, covered, 20 to 22 minutes for medium or until desired doneness is reached.

5. Place lamb on carving board. Slice between ribs with chef's knife into individual chops.

Makes 4 servings

Step 1. Pouring marinade over chops.

Step 3. Spreading mustard mixture over meaty side of lamb.

Step 5. Slicing lamb between ribs into individual chops.

Rosemary-Crusted Leg of Lamb

2 large cloves garlic
¼ cup Dijon-style mustard
1 boneless butterflied leg of lamb
(sirloin half, about 2½
pounds), well trimmed
3 tablespoons chopped fresh
rosemary leaves *or* **1**
tablespoon dried rosemary
leaves, crushed
Fresh rosemary sprigs
(optional)
Mint jelly (optional)

1. Prepare barbecue grill for direct cooking.

2. Meanwhile, to mince garlic, trim off ends of garlic cloves. Slightly crush cloves under flat side of chef's knife blade; peel away skin. Chop garlic with chef's knife until garlic is in uniform fine pieces.

3. Combine mustard and garlic in small bowl; spread half of mixture with fingers or spatula over one side of lamb. Sprinkle with half of chopped rosemary; pat into mustard mixture. Turn lamb over; repeat with remaining mustard mixture and rosemary.

4. Insert meat thermometer into center of thickest part of lamb.

5. Place lamb on grid. Grill lamb, on covered grill, over medium coals 35 to 40 minutes or until thermometer registers 160°F for medium or until desired doneness is reached, turning every 10 minutes.

6. Meanwhile, soak rosemary sprigs in water. Place rosemary sprigs directly on coals during last 10 minutes of grilling.

7. Transfer lamb to carving board; tent with foil. Let stand 10 minutes before carving into thin slices. Serve with mint jelly.

Makes 8 servings

Step 2. Crushing garlic clove to remove peel.

Step 3. Patting rosemary into mustard mixture.

Step 7. Carving lamb into thin slices.

Grilled Salmon with Cilantro Butter

Cilantro
1 clove garlic, peeled
¼ cup butter or margarine, softened
½ teaspoon grated lime or lemon peel (technique on page 81)
¼ teaspoon pepper
4 salmon fillets (about 6 ounces each)
Salt (optional)
Lime or lemon wedges

1. Rinse cilantro under cold running water. Pat dry with paper towels. Pull leaves off stems. Discard any wilted or bruised leaves. Tear off enough leaves to measure ⅓ cup packed.

2. Drop garlic clove through feed tube of food processor with motor running. Add cilantro leaves; process until cilantro is coarsely chopped.

3. Add butter, lime peel and pepper to cilantro mixture; process until well combined and cilantro is finely chopped.

4. Place butter mixture on sheet of waxed paper. Using waxed paper as a guide, roll mixture back and forth into 1-inch-diameter log, 2 inches long.

5. Wrap waxed paper around butter mixture to seal; refrigerate until firm, about 30 minutes.

6. Meanwhile, prepare barbecue grill for direct cooking.

7. Lightly sprinkle salmon with salt. Place salmon, skin-side down, on grid. Grill salmon, on covered grill, over medium coals 8 to 10 minutes or until salmon flakes easily when tested with fork.

8. Transfer salmon to serving plates. Cut butter log crosswise into 8 slices; top each fillet with 2 slices. Serve with lime or lemon wedges. *Makes 4 servings*

Step 1. Pulling cilantro leaves off stems.

Step 2. Processing cilantro leaves in food processor until coarsely chopped.

Step 4. Using waxed paper to roll butter mixture into log.

Szechuan Tuna Steaks

1 clove garlic
4 tuna steaks (6 ounces each), cut
   1 inch thick
¼ cup soy sauce
¼ cup dry sherry or sake
1 tablespoon Oriental sesame oil
1 teaspoon hot chili oil *or* ¼
   teaspoon crushed red pepper
3 tablespoons chopped cilantro

1. To mince garlic, trim off ends of garlic clove. Slightly crush clove under flat side of chef's knife blade; peel away skin. Chop garlic with chef's knife until garlic is in uniform fine pieces.

2. Place tuna in single layer in large shallow dish. Combine soy sauce, sherry, sesame oil, hot chili oil and garlic in small bowl. Reserve ¼ cup soy sauce mixture at room temperature. Pour remaining soy sauce mixture over tuna. Cover; marinate in refrigerator 40 minutes, turning once.

3. Prepare barbecue grill for direct cooking.

4. Drain tuna; discard marinade from dish. Place tuna on grid. Grill tuna, on uncovered grill, over medium-hot coals 6 minutes or until tuna is opaque, but still feels somewhat soft in center,* turning halfway through grilling time.

5. Transfer tuna to carving board. Cut each tuna steak into thin slices; fan out slices onto serving plates.

6. Drizzle tuna slices with reserved marinade; sprinkle with cilantro.   *Makes 4 servings*

*Tuna becomes dry and tough if overcooked. Tuna should be cooked as if it were beef.

Step 1. Crushing garlic clove to remove peel.

Step 2. Pouring soy sauce mixture over tuna steaks.

Step 5. Cutting tuna steak into thin slices.

Blackened Sea Bass

Hardwood charcoal*
2 teaspoons paprika
1 teaspoon garlic salt
**1 teaspoon dried thyme leaves,
  crushed**
¼ teaspoon ground white pepper
¼ teaspoon ground red pepper
¼ teaspoon ground black pepper
**3 tablespoons butter or
  margarine**
**4 skinless sea bass or catfish
  fillets (4 to 6 ounces each)**
Lemon halves
Fresh dill sprigs for garnish

*Hardwood charcoal takes somewhat longer than regular charcoal to become hot, but results in a hotter fire than regular charcoal. A hot fire is necessary to seal in the juices and cook fish quickly. If hardwood charcoal is not available, scatter dry hardwood, mesquite or hickory chunks over hot coals to create a hot fire.

1. Prepare barbecue grill for direct cooking using hardwood charcoal.

2. Meanwhile, combine paprika, garlic salt, thyme and white, red and black peppers in small bowl; mix well. Set aside.

3. Melt butter in small saucepan over medium heat. Pour melted butter into pie plate or shallow bowl. Cool slightly.

4. Dip sea bass into melted butter, evenly coating both sides.

5. Sprinkle both sides of sea bass evenly with paprika mixture.

6. Place sea bass on grid. (Fire will flare up when sea bass is placed on grid, but will subside when grill is covered.) Grill sea bass, on covered grill, over hot coals 4 to 6 minutes or until sea bass is blackened and flakes easily when tested with fork, turning halfway through grilling time. Serve with lemon halves. Garnish, if desired.

Makes 4 servings

Step 2. Combining paprika mixture.

Step 4. Dipping sea bass into melted butter.

Step 5. Sprinkling sea bass with paprika mixture.

Shanghai Fish Packets

1 small piece fresh ginger
4 orange roughy or tilefish fillets
   (4 to 6 ounces each)
¼ cup mirin* or Rhine wine
3 tablespoons soy sauce
1 tablespoon Oriental sesame oil
¼ teaspoon crushed red pepper
1 package (10 ounces) fresh
   spinach leaves
1 tablespoon peanut or vegetable
   oil
1 clove garlic, minced (technique
   on page 26)

*Mirin is a Japanese sweet wine available
in Japanese markets and the gourmet
section of large supermarkets.

1. Prepare barbecue grill for direct cooking.

2. To grate ginger, remove tough outer skin with sharp knife or vegetable peeler. Grate ginger using ginger grater or finest side of box-shaped grater. Grate enough ginger to measure 1½ teaspoons. Set aside.

3. Place orange roughy in single layer in large shallow dish. Combine mirin, soy sauce, sesame oil, ginger and crushed red pepper in small bowl; pour over orange roughy. Cover; marinate in refrigerator while preparing spinach.

4. Swish spinach leaves in cold water. Repeat several times with fresh cold water to remove sand and grit. Pat dry with paper towels.

5. Meanwhile, to remove stems from spinach leaves, fold each leaf in half, then with hand pull stem toward top of leaf. Discard stem.

6. Heat peanut oil in large skillet over medium heat. Add garlic; cook and stir 1 minute. Add spinach; cook and stir until wilted, about 3 minutes, tossing with 2 wooden spoons.

7. Place spinach mixture in center of four 12×12-inch squares of heavy-duty foil. Remove orange roughy from marinade; reserve marinade. Place 1 orange roughy fillet over each mound of spinach. Drizzle reserved marinade evenly over orange roughy. Wrap in foil using Drugstore Wrap technique. (Technique on page 10.)

8. Place packets on grid. Grill packets, on covered grill, over medium coals 15 to 18 minutes or until orange roughy flakes easily when tested with fork. *Makes 4 servings*

Step 2. Grating fresh ginger.

Step 4. Swishing spinach leaves in cold water to remove sand and grit.

Step 5. Pulling spinach stem toward top of leaf to remove.

Mediterranean Grilled Snapper

1 whole red snapper (about
   4½ pounds), scaled, gutted
   and cavity cut open*
2 tablespoons fresh lemon juice
   Salt and pepper
3 tablespoons olive oil, divided
2 tablespoons chopped fresh
   oregano leaves *or* 2 teaspoons
   dried oregano leaves, crushed
2 tablespoons chopped fresh basil
   leaves *or* 2 teaspoons dried
   basil leaves, crushed
4 slices lemon
1 metal skewer (6 inches long)
3 whole heads garlic**
   Hinged fish basket (optional)
   Fresh oregano sprigs (optional)
6 slices Italian bread, cut 1 inch
   thick
   Additional olive oil (optional)

*This can be done by your fish retailer at
the time of purchase or you may wish to
do this yourself.

**The whole garlic bulb is called a head.

1. Prepare barbecue grill for direct cooking.

2. Rinse snapper under cold running water;
pat dry with paper towels. Open cavity of
snapper; brush with lemon juice. Sprinkle
lightly with salt and pepper. Combine 1
tablespoon oil, chopped oregano and basil in
small bowl. Using small spatula, spread
mixture inside cavity of snapper.

3. Place lemon slices in cavity; close snapper.
Secure opening by threading skewer
lengthwise through outside edge of cavity.

4. Cut off top third of garlic heads to expose
cloves; discard. Place each head on small sheet
of heavy-duty foil; drizzle evenly with
remaining 2 tablespoons oil. Wrap in foil
using Drugstore Wrap technique. (Technique
on page 10.) Place packets directly on
medium-hot coals.

continued on page 56

Step 2. Spreading oil and herb
mixture inside cavity of snapper.

Step 3. Threading skewer
through outside edge of cavity to
secure.

Step 4. Cutting off top third of
garlic heads.

Mediterranean Grilled Snapper, continued

5. Place snapper in oiled, hinged fish basket or directly on oiled grid. Grill snapper and garlic, on uncovered grill, over medium-hot coals 20 to 25 minutes or until snapper flakes easily when tested with fork, turning halfway through grilling time.

6. Meanwhile, soak oregano sprigs in water. Place oregano sprigs directly on coals during last 10 minutes of grilling.

7. Brush bread lightly with additional oil. During last 5 minutes of grilling, place bread around outer edges of grid to toast, about 4 minutes, turning once.

8. Transfer snapper to carving board. Carefully unwrap garlic. Peel off any charred papery outer skin. Using pot holder, squeeze softened garlic from heads into small bowl; mash to a paste with wooden spoon or potato masher, adding additional oil. Spread bread lightly with garlic paste.

9. Remove skewer from snapper. Slit skin from head to tail along the back and belly of snapper; pull skin from top side of snapper with fingers. Discard skin.

10. Using utility knife, separate top fillet from backbone; cut into serving-size pieces. Lift up tail; pull forward to free backbone from lower fillet. Cut lower fillet into serving-size pieces. Remove skin, if desired.

Makes 6 servings

Note: A whole red snapper may not fit in a hinged fish basket. If desired, remove head and tail from snapper.

Step 7. Placing bread around outer edges of grid to toast.

Step 8. Squeezing softened garlic from heads.

Step 9. Pulling skin from top side of snapper.

Grilled Shrimp Creole

1 can (15 to 16 ounces) red beans
1½ pounds raw large shrimp
½ cup olive oil, divided
3 tablespoons balsamic or red wine vinegar
3 cloves garlic, minced, divided (technique on page 26)
3 tablespoons all-purpose flour
1 medium green bell pepper, coarsely chopped
1 medium onion, coarsely chopped
2 ribs celery, sliced
1 can (28 ounces) tomatoes, undrained, coarsely chopped
1 bay leaf
1½ teaspoons dried thyme leaves, crushed
¾ teaspoon hot pepper sauce
1 cup uncooked white rice, preferably converted
1 can (about 14 ounces) chicken broth
   Hinged grill basket or 6 metal skewers (12 inches long)
¼ cup chopped fresh parsley

1. Place beans in strainer. Rinse under cold running water; drain. Set aside.

2. To peel shrimp, remove the legs by gently pulling them off the shell. Loosen shell with fingers, then slide off.

3. To devein shrimp, with paring knife, cut a shallow slit along back of shrimp. Lift out vein. (You may find this easier to do under cold running water.) Place shrimp in shallow glass dish.

4. Combine ¼ cup oil, vinegar and 1 clove garlic in small bowl. Pour over shrimp; toss lightly to coat. Cover; marinate in refrigerator at least 30 minutes or up to 8 hours, turning occasionally.

continued on page 58

Step 1. Rinsing beans under cold running water.

Step 2. Removing shells from shrimp.

Step 3. Deveining shrimp.

Grilled Shrimp Creole, continued

5. For tomato sauce, heat remaining ¼ cup oil in large skillet over medium heat. Stir in flour. Cook and stir until flour is dark golden brown, 10 to 12 minutes.

6. Add bell pepper, onion, celery and remaining 2 cloves garlic; cook and stir 5 minutes. Add tomatoes with juice, bay leaf, thyme and hot pepper sauce. Simmer, uncovered, 25 to 30 minutes or until sauce has thickened and vegetables are fork-tender, stirring occasionally.*

7. Meanwhile, prepare barbecue grill for direct cooking.

8. While coals are heating, prepare rice according to package directions, substituting broth for 1¾ cups water and omitting salt. Stir in beans during last 5 minutes of cooking.

9. Drain shrimp; discard marinade. Place shrimp in grill basket or thread onto skewers. Place grill basket or skewers on grid. Grill shrimp, on uncovered grill, over medium coals 6 to 8 minutes or until shrimp are opaque, turning halfway through grilling time.

10. Remove bay leaf from tomato sauce. Arrange rice and beans on 4 serving plates; top with tomato sauce. Remove shrimp from grill basket or skewers. Arrange shrimp over tomato sauce. Sprinkle with parsley.

Makes 4 servings

*If desired, tomato sauce may be prepared up to 1 day ahead. Cover and refrigerate. Reheat sauce in medium saucepan over medium heat while shrimp are grilling.

Step 5. Cooking and stirring oil and flour until flour is dark golden brown.

Step 6. Cooking and stirring bell pepper, onion, celery and garlic.

Step 9. Grilling shrimp in grill basket until shrimp are opaque.

Seafood Kabobs

Nonstick cooking spray
1 pound raw large shrimp, peeled, deveined (technique on page 57)
10 ounces skinless swordfish or halibut steaks, cut 1 inch thick
2 tablespoons honey mustard
2 teaspoons fresh lemon juice
8 metal skewers (12 inches long)
8 slices bacon (regular slice, not thick)
Lemon wedges (optional)

1. Spray room temperature barbecue grid with nonstick cooking spray. Prepare barbecue grill for direct cooking.

2. Place shrimp in shallow glass dish. Cut swordfish into 1-inch cubes on cutting board; add to shrimp in dish.

3. Combine honey mustard and lemon juice in small bowl. Pour over shrimp mixture; toss lightly to coat.

4. To assemble skewers, pierce skewer through 1 end of bacon slice. Add 1 piece shrimp. Pierce skewer through bacon slice again, wrapping bacon slice around 1 side of shrimp.

5. Add 1 piece swordfish. Pierce bacon slice again, wrapping bacon around opposite side of swordfish. Continue adding seafood and wrapping with bacon, pushing ingredients to middle of skewer until end of bacon slice is reached. Repeat with remaining skewers. Brush any remaining mustard mixture over skewers.

6. Place skewers on grid. Grill skewers, on covered grill, over medium coals 8 to 10 minutes or until shrimp are opaque and swordfish flakes easily when tested with fork, turning halfway through grilling time. Serve with lemon wedges.   *Makes 4 servings (2 kabobs per serving)*

Note: Kabobs can be prepared up to 3 hours before grilling. Cover and refrigerate until ready to grill.

Step 2. Cutting swordfish into 1-inch cubes.

Step 4. Wrapping bacon slice around 1 side of shrimp.

Step 5. Wrapping bacon slice around opposite side of swordfish.

Glazed Cornish Hens

1 small piece fresh ginger
2 fresh or thawed frozen Cornish game hens (1½ pounds each)
3 tablespoons fresh lemon juice
1 large clove garlic, minced (technique on page 26)
¼ cup orange marmalade
1 tablespoon coarse-grain or country-style mustard

1. To grate ginger, remove tough outer skin with sharp knife or vegetable peeler. Grate ginger using ginger grater or the finest side of box-shaped grater. Grate enough ginger to measure 2 teaspoons. Set aside.

2. Remove giblets from cavities of hens; reserve for another use. Split hens in half on cutting board with sharp knife or poultry shears, cutting through breast and back bones. Rinse hens with cold water; pat dry with paper towels. Place hen halves in large resealable plastic food storage bag.

3. Combine lemon juice and garlic in small bowl; pour over hens in bag. Seal bag tightly, turning to coat. Marinate in refrigerator 30 minutes.

4. Meanwhile, prepare barbecue grill for direct cooking.

5. Drain hens; discard marinade.

6. Place hens, skin-sides up, on grid. Grill hens, on covered grill, over medium-hot coals 20 minutes.

7. Meanwhile, combine marmalade, mustard and ginger in small bowl. Brush half of mixture evenly over hens. Continue to grill, covered, 10 minutes. Brush with remaining mixture. Continue to grill, covered, 5 to 10 minutes or until thighs move easily and juices run clear. *Makes 4 servings*

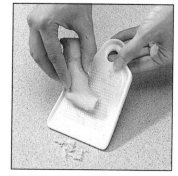

Step 1. Grating fresh ginger.

Step 2. Splitting hen in half through breast and back bone.

Step 7. Brushing marmalade mixture over hens.

Grilled Chicken Caesar Salad

1 pound boneless skinless chicken
  breast halves
½ cup extra-virgin olive oil
3 tablespoons fresh lemon juice
2 teaspoons anchovy paste
2 cloves garlic, minced (technique
  on page 26)
½ teaspoon salt
½ teaspoon pepper
6 cups torn washed romaine
  lettuce leaves (technique on
  page 12)
4 plum tomatoes, quartered
¼ cup grated Parmesan cheese
1 cup purchased garlic croutons
  Anchovy fillets (optional)
  Additional pepper (optional)

1. Place chicken in large resealable plastic food storage bag. Combine oil, lemon juice, anchovy paste, garlic, salt and ½ teaspoon pepper in small bowl. Reserve ⅓ cup of marinade; cover and refrigerate until serving. Pour remaining marinade over chicken in bag. Seal bag tightly, turning to coat. Marinate in refrigerator at least 1 hour or up to 4 hours, turning occasionally.

2. Combine lettuce, tomatoes and cheese in large bowl. Cover; refrigerate until serving.

3. Prepare barbecue grill for direct cooking.

4. Drain chicken; reserve marinade from bag. Place chicken on grid. Grill chicken, on covered grill, over medium coals 10 to 12 minutes or until chicken is no longer pink in center, brushing with reserved marinade from bag after 5 minutes and turning halfway through grilling time. Discard remaining marinade from bag. Cool chicken slightly.

5. Slice warm chicken crosswise into ½-inch-wide strips; add chicken and croutons to lettuce mixture in bowl. Drizzle with ⅓ cup reserved marinade; toss to coat well. Top with anchovy fillets and serve with additional pepper. *Makes 4 servings*

Note: Chicken may also be refrigerated until cold before slicing.

Step 1. Pouring remaining marinade over chicken.

Step 4. Brushing chicken with reserved marinade.

Step 5. Slicing chicken crosswise into ½-inch-wide strips.

Grilled Chicken Tostadas

1 head romaine lettuce
1 medium tomato
1 pound boneless skinless chicken
    breast halves
1 teaspoon ground cumin
¼ cup fresh orange juice
    (technique on page 81)
¼ cup plus 2 tablespoons
    purchased hot or mild salsa,
    divided
1 tablespoon vegetable oil
2 cloves garlic, minced (technique
    on page 26)
8 green onions
    Additional vegetable oil
1 can (16 ounces) refried beans
4 (10-inch) or 8 (6- to 7-inch)
    flour tortillas
1½ cups (6 ounces) shredded
    Monterey Jack cheese with
    jalapeño peppers
1 ripe medium avocado, pitted
    and diced (optional, technique
    on page 16)
    Chopped cilantro (optional)
    Sour cream

1. Wash lettuce in several changes of cold water. Drain well and pat dry with paper towels to remove excess moisture, if necessary. Or, spin in salad spinner to remove moisture.

2. Discard any wilted or bruised leaves. Cut or tear off stems if they are woody.

3. Stack several lettuce leaves on cutting board. Cut stack lengthwise in half. Stack one section on top of the other. Cut stack crosswise into very thin slices. Slice enough lettuce to measure 2 cups. Set aside.

4. To seed tomato, cut tomato in half horizontally. Hold each tomato half over bowl, cut side down, and squeeze to remove seeds. Coarsely chop tomato with chef's knife. Set aside.

continued on page 68

Step 1. Spinning greens in salad spinner.

Step 3. Cutting lettuce crosswise into very thin slices.

Step 4. Squeezing tomato half to remove seeds.

Grilled Chicken Tostadas, continued

5. Place chicken in single layer in shallow glass dish; sprinkle with cumin. Combine orange juice, ¼ cup salsa, 1 tablespoon oil and garlic in small bowl; pour over chicken. Cover; marinate in refrigerator at least 2 hours or up to 8 hours, stirring mixture occasionally.

6. Prepare barbecue grill for direct cooking.

7. Drain chicken; reserve marinade. Brush green onions with additional oil. Place chicken and green onions on grid. Grill, on covered grill, over medium-hot coals 5 minutes. Brush tops of chicken with half of reserved marinade; turn and brush with remaining marinade. Turn onions. Continue to grill, covered, 5 minutes or until chicken is no longer pink in center and onions are tender. (If onions are browning too quickly, remove before chicken is done.)

8. Meanwhile, combine beans and remaining 2 tablespoons salsa in small saucepan; cook, stirring occasionally, over medium heat until hot.

9. Place tortillas in single layer on grid. Grill tortillas, on uncovered grill, 1 to 2 minutes per side or until golden brown. (If tortillas puff up, pierce with tip of knife or flatten by pressing with spatula.)

10. Transfer chicken and onions to carving board. Slice chicken crosswise into ½-inch-wide strips. Cut green onions crosswise into 1-inch-long pieces. Spread tortillas with bean mixture; top with lettuce, chicken, onions, cheese, avocado and tomato. Sprinkle with cilantro. Serve with sour cream.

Makes 4 servings

Step 7. Brushing tops of chicken with reserved marinade.

Step 9. Piercing tortilla with tip of knife to flatten.

Step 10. Slicing chicken crosswise into ½-inch-wide strips.

Pesto-Stuffed Grilled Chicken

2 tablespoons pine nuts or
   walnuts
   Fresh basil leaves
2 cloves garlic, peeled
¼ teaspoon pepper
5 tablespoons extra-virgin olive
   oil, divided
¼ cup grated Parmesan cheese
1 fresh or thawed frozen roasting
   chicken or capon (6 to 7
   pounds)
2 tablespoons fresh lemon juice
   Additional fresh basil leaves
   and fresh red currants for
   garnish

1. To toast pine nuts, spread in single layer on baking sheet. Bake in preheated 350°F oven 8 to 10 minutes or until golden brown, stirring frequently. Remove pine nuts from baking sheet; cool completely. Set aside.

2. Rinse basil leaves under cold running water. Remove stems; discard. Pat leaves dry with paper towel. Prepare enough basil leaves to measure ½ cup packed. Set aside.

3. Meanwhile, prepare barbecue grill with rectangular metal or foil drip pan. Bank briquets on either side of drip pan for indirect cooking.

4. To prepare pesto, drop garlic cloves through feed tube of food processor with motor running. Add basil, pine nuts and pepper; process until basil is minced. With processor running, add 3 tablespoons oil in slow, steady stream until smooth paste forms, scraping down side of bowl once. Add cheese; process until well blended.

continued on page 70

Step 1. Toasting pine nuts until golden brown.

Step 2. Removing stems from basil leaves.

Step 4. Processing pesto in food processor until well blended.

***Pesto-Stuffed Grilled Chicken,
continued***

5. Remove giblets from chicken cavity; reserve for another use. Rinse chicken with cold water; pat dry with paper towels. Loosen skin over breast of chicken by pushing fingers between skin and meat, taking care not to tear skin. Do not loosen skin over wings and drumsticks.

6. Using rubber spatula or small spoon, spread pesto under breast skin; massage skin to evenly spread pesto.

7. Combine remaining 2 tablespoons oil and lemon juice in small bowl; brush over chicken skin.

8. Insert meat thermometer into center of thickest part of thigh, not touching bone.

9. Tuck wings under back; tie legs together with wet kitchen string. Place chicken, breast-side up, on grid directly over drip pan. Grill chicken, on covered grill, over medium-low coals 1 hour 10 minutes to 1 hour 30 minutes or until thermometer registers 185°F, adding 4 to 9 briquets to both sides of the fire after 45 minutes to maintain medium-low coals.

10. Transfer chicken to carving board; tent with foil. Let stand 15 minutes before carving. Garnish, if desired.

Makes 6 servings

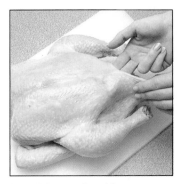

Step 5. Loosening skin over chicken breast by pushing fingers between skin and meat.

Step 6. Spreading pesto under breast skin.

Step 8. Inserting meat thermometer into thickest part of thigh, not touching bone.

Buffalo Chicken Drumsticks

1 clove garlic
8 large chicken drumsticks
    (about 2 pounds)
3 tablespoons hot pepper sauce
1 tablespoon vegetable oil
¼ cup mayonnaise
3 tablespoons sour cream
1½ tablespoons white wine vinegar
¼ teaspoon sugar
⅓ cup (1½ ounces) crumbled
    Roquefort or blue cheese
2 cups hickory chips
    Celery sticks

1. To mince garlic, trim off ends of garlic clove. Slightly crush clove under flat side of chef's knife blade; peel away skin. Chop garlic with chef's knife until garlic is in uniform fine pieces.

2. Place chicken in large resealable plastic food storage bag. Combine hot pepper sauce, oil and garlic in small bowl; pour over chicken. Seal bag tightly, turning to coat. Marinate in refrigerator at least 1 hour or, for hotter flavor, up to 24 hours, turning occasionally.

3. For blue cheese dressing, combine mayonnaise, sour cream, vinegar and sugar in another small bowl. Stir in cheese; cover and refrigerate until serving.

4. Prepare barbecue grill for direct cooking.

5. Meanwhile, cover hickory chips with cold water; soak 20 minutes.

6. Drain chicken; discard marinade. Drain hickory chips; sprinkle over coals.

7. Place chicken on grid. Grill chicken, on covered grill, over medium-hot coals 25 to 30 minutes or until chicken is no longer pink in center and juices run clear, turning 3 to 4 times. Serve with blue cheese dressing and celery sticks. *Makes 4 servings*

Step 2. Pouring marinade over chicken.

Step 5. Covering hickory chips with cold water to soak.

Step 6. Sprinkling hickory chips over coals.

Thai Satay Chicken Skewers

1 pound boneless skinless chicken breast halves
⅓ cup soy sauce
2 tablespoons fresh lime juice (technique on page 39)
2 cloves garlic, minced (technique on page 26)
1 teaspoon grated fresh ginger (technique on page 62)
¾ teaspoon crushed red pepper
2 tablespoons water
8 bamboo skewers (10 to 12 inches long)
¾ cup canned unsweetened coconut milk
1 tablespoon creamy peanut butter
4 green onions with tops, cleaned and cut into 1-inch pieces

1. Slice chicken crosswise into ⅜-inch-wide strips; place in shallow glass dish.

2. Combine soy sauce, lime juice, garlic, ginger and crushed red pepper in small bowl. Reserve 3 tablespoons marinade; cover and refrigerate until preparing peanut sauce. Add water to remaining marinade. Pour over chicken; toss to coat well. Cover; marinate in refrigerator at least 30 minutes or up to 2 hours, stirring mixture occasionally.

3. Cover bamboo skewers with cold water. Soak 20 minutes to prevent them from burning; drain.

4. Prepare barbecue grill for direct cooking.

5. Meanwhile, for peanut sauce, combine coconut milk, reserved soy sauce mixture and peanut butter in small saucepan. Bring to a boil over medium-high heat, stirring constantly. Reduce heat to low and simmer, uncovered, 2 to 4 minutes or until sauce thickens. Keep warm.

6. Drain chicken; reserve marinade from dish. Weave 3 to 4 chicken pieces accordion style onto each skewer, alternating with green onion pieces placed crosswise on skewer. Brush reserved marinade from dish over chicken and onions. Discard remaining marinade.

7. Place skewers on grid. Grill skewers, on uncovered grill, over medium-hot coals 6 to 8 minutes or until chicken is no longer pink in center, turning halfway through grilling time. Serve with warm peanut sauce for dipping.

Makes 4 servings

Step 2. Adding water to remaining marinade.

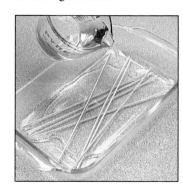

Step 3. Covering bamboo skewers with cold water to soak.

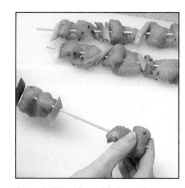

Step 6. Weaving chicken pieces accordion style onto skewer.

Maple-Glazed Turkey Breast

1 orange
1 bone-in turkey breast (5 to 6 pounds)
Roast rack (optional)
¼ cup pure maple syrup
2 tablespoons butter or margarine, melted
1 tablespoon bourbon (optional)
Fresh bay leaves for garnish

1. Prepare barbecue grill with rectangular metal or foil drip pan. Bank briquets on either side of drip pan for indirect cooking.

2. Meanwhile, to grate orange peel, rinse orange under running water. Grate orange peel using the finest side of box-shaped grater, being careful to remove only the outermost layer of skin and not any of the bitter white pith. Grate enough peel to measure 2 teaspoons. Set aside.

3. Insert meat thermometer into center of thickest part of turkey breast, not touching bone.

4. Place turkey, bone-side down, on roast rack or directly on grid, directly over drip pan. Grill turkey, on covered grill, over medium coals 55 minutes, adding 4 to 9 briquets to both sides of the fire after 45 minutes to maintain medium coals.

5. Combine maple syrup, butter, bourbon and orange peel in small bowl; brush half of mixture over turkey. Continue to grill, covered, 10 minutes. Brush with remaining mixture; continue to grill, covered, about 10 minutes or until thermometer registers 170°F.

6. Transfer turkey to carving board; tent with foil. Let stand 10 minutes before carving. Cut turkey into thin slices. Garnish, if desired.

Makes 6 to 8 servings

Variation: For hickory-smoked flavor, cover 2 cups hickory chips with cold water; soak 20 minutes. Drain; sprinkle over coals just before placing turkey on grid.

Step 2. Grating orange peel using finest side of box-shaped grater.

Step 3. Inserting meat thermometer into center of thickest part of turkey breast.

Step 6. Carving turkey into thin slices.

Mesquite-Grilled Turkey

2 cups mesquite chips, divided
2 cloves garlic
1 fresh or thawed frozen turkey
**   (10 to 12 pounds)**
1 small sweet or Spanish onion,
**   peeled and quartered**
1 lemon, quartered
3 fresh tarragon sprigs
1 metal skewer (6 inches long)
2 tablespoons butter or
**   margarine, softened**
**   Salt and pepper (optional)**
¼ cup butter or margarine,
**   melted**
**   Additional fresh tarragon**
**   sprigs (optional)**
2 tablespoons fresh lemon juice
2 tablespoons chopped fresh
**   tarragon leaves *or* 2 teaspoons**
**   dried tarragon leaves, crushed**

1. Prepare barbecue grill with rectangular metal or foil drip pan. Bank briquets on either side of drip pan for indirect cooking.

2. Meanwhile, cover mesquite chips with cold water; soak 20 minutes.

3. To mince garlic, trim off ends of garlic cloves. Slightly crush cloves under flat side of chef's knife blade; peel away skin. Chop garlic with chef's knife until garlic is in uniform fine pieces.

4. Remove giblets from turkey cavity; reserve for another use. Rinse turkey with cold running water; pat dry with paper towels. Place onion, lemon and 3 tarragon sprigs in cavity. Pull skin over neck; secure with metal skewer. Tuck wing tips under back; tie legs together with wet kitchen string.

5. Using fingers or paper towel, spread softened butter over turkey skin; sprinkle with salt and pepper to taste.

continued on page 80

Step 2. Covering mesquite chips with cold water to soak.

Step 4. Securing skin pulled over neck with metal skewer.

Step 5. Spreading softened butter over turkey skin.

6. Insert meat thermometer into center of thickest part of thigh, not touching bone.

7. Drain mesquite chips; sprinkle 1 cup over coals. Place turkey, breast-side up, on grid directly over drip pan. Grill turkey, on covered grill, over medium coals 11 to 14 minutes per pound, adding 4 to 9 briquets to both sides of the fire each hour to maintain medium coals and adding remaining 1 cup mesquite chips after 1 hour of grilling.

8. Meanwhile, soak additional fresh tarragon sprigs in water.

9. Combine melted butter, lemon juice, chopped tarragon and garlic in small bowl. Brush half of mixture over turkey during last 30 minutes of grilling. Place soaked tarragon sprigs directly on coals. Continue to grill, covered, 20 minutes. Brush with remaining mixture. Continue to grill, covered, about 10 minutes or until thermometer registers 185°F.

10. Transfer turkey to carving board; tent with foil. Let stand 15 minutes before carving. Discard onion, lemon and tarragon sprigs from cavity.

Makes 8 to 10 servings

Step 6. Inserting meat thermometer into thickest part of thigh, not touching bone.

Step 7. Adding additional briquets to fire to maintain medium coals.

Three-Citrus Turkey Tenderloins

2 medium oranges
1 large lemon
1 large lime
3 tablespoons minced shallots or
    onion
2 whole turkey tenderloins (about
    ¾ pound each)
1 tablespoon olive oil
½ teaspoon salt
2½ tablespoons honey
1 teaspoon cornstarch

1. To juice oranges, cut oranges in half on cutting board; with tip of knife, remove any visible seeds.

2. Using citrus reamer or squeezing tightly with hand, squeeze juice from oranges into small bowl. Remove any remaining seeds from bowl. Squeeze enough juice to measure ⅔ cup. Set aside.

3. To grate lemon peel, rinse lemon under running water. Grate lemon peel using the finest side of box-shaped grater, being careful to remove only the outermost layer of skin and not any of the bitter, white pith. Grate enough peel to measure ½ teaspoon. Set aside.

4. Repeat juicing technique with lemon. Squeeze enough lemon juice to measure 2 tablespoons. Set aside.

5. Repeat grating technique with lime. Grate enough lime peel to measure ½ teaspoon. Set aside.

continued on page 82

Step 1. Removing seeds from orange.

Step 2. Squeezing juice from orange.

Step 3. Grating lemon peel using finest side of box-shaped grater.

Three-Citrus Turkey Tenderloins,
continued

6. Repeat juicing technique with lime. Squeeze enough lime juice to measure 2 tablespoons.

7. Combine ⅓ cup orange juice, shallots, lemon peel, lemon juice, lime peel and lime juice in small bowl; mix well. Reserve ⅓ cup of juice mixture; cover and refrigerate. Place turkey in large resealable plastic food storage bag; add remaining juice mixture to bag. Seal bag tightly, turning to coat. Marinate in refrigerator 1 to 2 hours, turning once.

8. Prepare barbecue grill for direct cooking.

9. Drain turkey; discard marinade from bag. Brush turkey with oil; sprinkle with salt. Place turkey on grid. Grill turkey, on covered grill, over medium-hot coals 15 to 20 minutes or until no longer pink in center, turning halfway through grilling time. (If desired, insert instant-read thermometer* into center of thickest part of tenderloin. Thermometer should register 170°F.)

10. Meanwhile, combine reserved juice mixture and honey in small saucepan. Combine remaining ⅓ cup orange juice and cornstarch in small bowl; mix until smooth. Add to juice mixture in saucepan. Simmer, uncovered, over medium heat about 5 minutes or until thickened and reduced to ½ cup.

11. Transfer turkey to carving board. Carve turkey crosswise into thin slices; drizzle with sauce.

Makes 4 to 6 servings

*Do not leave instant-read thermometer in tenderloins during grilling since the thermometer is not heatproof.

Step 9. Inserting instant-read thermometer into center of thickest part of tenderloin.

Step 10. Adding combined orange juice and cornstarch to juice mixture in saucepan.

Step 11. Carving turkey crosswise into thin slices.

Grilled Cajun Potato Wedges

3 large russet potatoes
  (about 2¼ pounds)
¼ cup olive oil
2 cloves garlic, minced (technique
  on page 26)
1 teaspoon salt
1 teaspoon paprika
½ teaspoon dried thyme leaves,
  crushed
½ teaspoon dried oregano leaves,
  crushed
¼ teaspoon black pepper
⅛ to ¼ teaspoon ground red
  pepper
2 cups mesquite chips

1. Prepare barbecue grill for direct cooking. Preheat oven to 425°F.

2. To prepare potatoes, scrub potatoes under running water with stiff vegetable brush; rinse. Dry well. (Do not peel.)

3. Cut potatoes in half lengthwise with chef's knife; then cut each half lengthwise into 4 wedges.

4. Place potatoes in large bowl. Add oil and garlic; toss to coat well.

5. Combine salt, paprika, thyme, oregano, black pepper and ground red pepper in small bowl. Sprinkle over potatoes; toss to coat well.

6. Place potato wedges in single layer in shallow roasting pan. (Reserve remaining oil mixture left in large bowl.) Bake 20 minutes.

7. Meanwhile, cover mesquite chips with cold water; soak 20 minutes.

8. Drain mesquite chips; sprinkle over coals. Place potato wedges on their sides on grid. Grill potato wedges, on covered grill, over medium coals 15 to 20 minutes or until potatoes are browned and fork-tender, brushing with reserved oil mixture halfway through grilling time and turning once with tongs.   *Makes 4 to 6 servings*

Step 2. Scrubbing potatoes under running water with vegetable brush.

Step 3. Cutting potato halves lengthwise into 4 wedges.

Step 5. Sprinkling seasoning mixture over potatoes.

Grilled Coriander Corn

4 ears fresh corn
3 tablespoons butter or
margarine, softened
1 teaspoon ground coriander
¼ teaspoon salt (optional)
⅛ teaspoon ground red pepper

1. Pull outer husks from top to base of each ear of corn; leave husks attached to ear. (If desired, remove 1 strip of husk from inner portion of each ear; reserve for later use.)

2. Strip away silk from corn by hand. (Technique on page 40.)

3. Remove any remaining silk with dry vegetable brush. Trim any blemishes from corn. (Technique on page 40.)

4. Place corn in large bowl. Cover with cold water; soak 20 to 30 minutes.

5. Meanwhile, prepare barbecue grill for direct cooking.

6. Remove corn from water; pat kernels dry with paper towels. Combine butter, coriander, salt and ground red pepper in small bowl. Spread evenly with spatula over kernels.

7. Bring husks back up over each ear of corn; secure at top with paper-covered metal twist-ties. (Or, use reserved strips of corn husk to tie knots at the top of each ear, if desired.)

8. Place corn on grid. Grill corn, on covered grill, over medium-hot coals 20 to 25 minutes or until corn is hot and tender, turning halfway through grilling time with tongs.

Makes 4 servings

Note: For ember cooking, prepare corn as recipe directs, but omit soaking in cold water. Wrap each ear securely in heavy-duty foil. Place directly on coals. Grill corn, in covered grill, on medium-hot coals 25 to 30 minutes or until corn is hot and tender, turning every 10 minutes with tongs.

Step 1. Pulling outer husk to base of corn.

Step 5. Briquets arranged in grill for direct cooking.

Step 6. Spreading butter mixture over kernels.

Grilled Sweet Potato Packets with Pecan Butter

¼ cup chopped pecans
4 sweet potatoes (about 8 ounces each)
1 large sweet or Spanish onion, thinly sliced and separated into rings (technique on page 14)
3 tablespoons vegetable oil
⅓ cup butter or margarine, softened
2 tablespoons packed light brown sugar
¼ teaspoon salt
¼ teaspoon ground cinnamon

1. Prepare barbecue grill for direct cooking.

2. Meanwhile, to toast pecans, spread in single layer on baking sheet. Bake in preheated 350°F oven 8 to 10 minutes or until golden brown, stirring frequently. Remove pecans from baking sheet; cool to room temperature. Set aside.

3. To prepare sweet potatoes, peel with vegetable peeler.

4. Slice potatoes crosswise into ¼-inch-thick slices.

5. Alternately place potato slices and onion rings on four 14×12-inch sheets of heavy-duty foil. Brush tops and sides with oil to prevent drying.

6. Wrap in foil using Drugstore Wrap technique. (Technique on page 10.) Place foil packets on grid. Grill packets, on covered grill, over medium coals 25 to 30 minutes or until potatoes are fork-tender.

7. Meanwhile, to prepare Pecan Butter, combine butter, sugar, salt and cinnamon in small bowl; mix well. Stir in pecans. Open packets carefully; top each with dollop of Pecan Butter. *Makes 4 servings*

Step 2. Toasting pecans until golden brown.

Step 3. Peeling sweet potatoes.

Step 4. Slicing sweet potatoes crosswise into ¼-inch-thick slices.

Herbed Mushroom Vegetable Medley

4 ounces button or crimini
    mushrooms
1 medium red or yellow bell
    pepper, cut into ¼-inch-wide
    strips
1 medium zucchini, cut crosswise
    into ¼-inch-thick slices
1 medium yellow squash, cut
    crosswise into ¼-inch-thick
    slices
3 tablespoons butter or
    margarine, melted
1 tablespoon chopped fresh
    thyme leaves *or* 1 teaspoon
    dried thyme leaves, crushed
1 tablespoon chopped fresh basil
    leaves *or* 1 teaspoon dried
    basil leaves, crushed
1 tablespoon chopped fresh chives
    or green onion tops (technique
    on page 24)
1 clove garlic, minced (technique
    on page 26)
¼ teaspoon salt
¼ teaspoon black pepper

1. Prepare barbecue grill for direct cooking.

2. To prepare mushrooms, brush dirt from mushrooms; clean by wiping with damp paper towel.

3. Cut thin slice from base of each mushroom stem with paring knife; discard. Thinly slice mushroom stems and caps.

4. Combine mushrooms, bell pepper, zucchini and squash in large bowl. Combine butter, thyme, basil, chives, garlic, salt and black pepper in small bowl. Pour over vegetable mixture; toss to coat well.

5. Transfer mixture to 20×14-inch sheet of heavy-duty foil. Wrap in foil using Drugstore Wrap technique. (Technique on page 10.)

6. Place foil packet on grid. Grill packet, on covered grill, over medium coals 20 to 25 minutes or until vegetables are fork-tender. Open packet carefully to serve.

Makes 4 to 6 servings

Step 2. Wiping mushrooms with damp paper towel to clean.

Step 3. Cutting thin slice from base of mushroom stem.

Step 5. Wrapping vegetable mixture using Drugstore Wrap technique.

Grilled Tri-Colored Pepper Salad

Fresh basil leaves
1 each large red, yellow and
green bell pepper, cut into
halves or quarters
⅓ cup extra-virgin olive oil
3 tablespoons balsamic vinegar
2 cloves garlic, minced (technique
on page 26)
¼ teaspoon salt
¼ teaspoon black pepper
⅓ cup crumbled goat cheese
(about 1½ ounces)

1. Prepare barbecue grill for direct cooking.

2. Layer basil leaves with largest leaf on bottom, then roll up jelly-roll style. Slice basil roll into very thin slices; separate into strips. Slice enough leaves to measure ¼ cup. Set aside.

3. Place bell peppers, skin-side down, on grid. Grill bell peppers, on covered grill, over hot coals 10 to 12 minutes or until skin is charred.

4. To steam bell peppers and loosen skin, place charred bell peppers in paper bag. Close bag; set aside to cool 10 to 15 minutes.

5. To peel bell peppers, remove skin with paring knife; discard skin.

6. Place bell peppers in shallow glass serving dish. Combine oil, vinegar, garlic, salt and black pepper in small bowl; whisk until well combined. Pour over bell peppers. Let stand 30 minutes at room temperature. (Or, cover and refrigerate up to 24 hours. Bring bell peppers to room temperature before serving.)

7. Sprinkle bell peppers with cheese and basil just before serving.   *Makes 4 to 6 servings*

Step 2. Slicing basil roll into very thin slices.

Step 3. Grilling bell peppers until skin is charred.

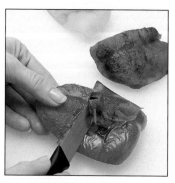

Step 5. Peeling bell peppers by removing skin with paring knife.

INDEX